THE REVERSE I CHING (WEST)

and/or

"The Reverse Book of the Easy"

by :

The Hopi Book Club

WEST   *8*

SOUTH   *28*

EAST   *48*

NORTH   *68*

"If a storm is coming ...

Then this is our counter-storm ..."

- The Legendary Kung Fu Novel

WEST

"A great tailor cuts little"

Paradox of Truth

High and Low

Not Serious

The Power of a Buck

The Wisdom of Constancy

Flexibility and Strength

Body

Paradox of Truth

Truth require few words
Words no describe truth

Therefore

The ancients say

"Truth can often sound paradoxical"

-Tao Te Ching

High and Low

You think too high of yourself
something likely go down
probably the part of you
that think too high

Others think too low of you
something likely go up
probably the part of them
that think too low

Therefore
The ancients say

"A great tailor cuts little"

-Tao Te Ching

Not Serious

You serious
You attract serious

Therefore

The ancients say

"Others sharp and clever
I alone dull and stupid"

-Tao Te Ching

The Power of a Buck

If you can stay at Hilton
For the same price as Motel 6

Which hotel is over priced?
Which under priced?

And if they both charge only a buck

Which you thank more?
Which thanks you more?

Therefore
The ancients say

"Learn not to hold onto ideas"

-Tao Te Ching

The Wisdom of Constancy

**When young
parents love nurture and no b.s.**

**When tides turn
children should treat them same**

Therefore

The ancients say

"Knowing constancy is insight"

-Tao Te Ching

Flexibility and Strength

40 on a 60 : are you too slow?
40 on a 20 : are you to fast?

World go one way
you move only one way?

World go other way
you move only other way?

Therefore
The ancients say

"Force is followed by loss of strength"

-Tao Te Ching

Body

**You rotate around sun
or sun move in your dream?**

**If sun move in your dream
You rotate around sun
Or sun rotate around you?**

**If sun rotate around you
Where is your body?**

**Therefore
The ancients say**

"Death no place to enter"

- Tao Te Ching

"Learn not to hold onto ideas"

SOUTH

"Humbling to force is power"

No Choice

The Little Engine Who Could

The Power of Humility

A Fool

Nothing to Lose

Root

Business

No Choice

**If storm coming
you have choice**

**If storm here
no choice**

Therefore

The saying

**"Like lion approaching
no choice You fear you suffer"**

The Little Engine Who Could

If you the little engine who could
but could not

That why they call you
The little engine who could

Therefore

The ancients say

"In dealing with weeds
Firm resolution necessary"

- The I Ching

The Power of Humility

Dragon humble to chicken

The mightier the dragon
The mightier the strength

Therefore

The ancients say

"Humbling to force is power"

-Tao Te Ching

A Fool

If monkey can act like a fool
All other monkeys can too

If all other monkeys act like fool
It would be called foolish
For that one monkey
To not act like a fool

Therefore

The ancients say

"Above not bright
Below not dark"

- Tao Te Ching

Nothing to Lose

Winner and/or loser ?
Saint and/or sinner ?

Which label
less to lose?

Therefore

The ancients say

"When wisdom and intelligence are
born the great pretense begins"

- Tao Te Ching

Root

**Anything imagine unreal
is one's imagination**

**Anything imagine real
is one's imagination**

**What is real then?
If one can imagine it
It is one's imagination**

Therefore

The ancients say

**"What is firmly established cannot
be uprooted"**

- Tao Te Ching

Business

Change and no change
Movement and constant

Shape change content same
Content change shape same

If both change
then compassion only anchor

Therefore

The ancients say

"In business, be competent
In action, watch the timing"

-Tao Te Ching

"Humbling to force is power"

EAST

"Know the value of non-action"

Better Doing

Generosity

Strangers and Friends

Love and sex

Don't Behave

The Power of Movement

Enough is Enough

Better Doing

Death sex and duty

Without duty
Duty perform better

Therefore

The ancients say

"Know the value of non-action"

-Tao Te Ching

Generosity

You lack
You lack

You no lack
You no lack

It is really that simple

Therefore

The ancients say

"From simplicity comes generosity"

-Tao Te Ching

Strangers and Friends

Self and others
Known and unknown

Less unknown
Less stranger
and more friends

Therefore

The saying

"Know thyself"

Love and sex

Chicken can love another chicken and have good sex with another chicken

Chicken can have bad sex and love the other chicken

Chicken can have good sex and not love the other chicken

**To the chicken farmer
It makes no difference**

**Therefore
The ancients say**

**"You find what you seek
and are forgiven when you sin
This the greatest treasure"**

-Tao Te Ching

Don't Behave

Chicken is attracted to chicken
Even if beautiful elephant near

If chicken leave elephants for other chickens
Elephants may think chicken did not behave

Therefore

The ancients say

"Like a newborn baby
With out direction
Like the restless wind"

-Tao Te Ching

The Power of Movement

Young and old
Stiff and flexible

Rejuvenate and degenerate
Less and more strength

Yield and not yield
Not move and move

Therefore

The ancients say

"The more it moves
The more it yields"

-Tao Te Ching

Enough is Enough

**Sickness and health
Comfort and discomfort
Hard and easy**

**Body know if it happy
Mind know if it happy
You may not**

Therefore

The ancients say

**"He who knows enough is enough
will always have enough"**

-Tao Te Ching

Enough Is Enough

Sickness and health,
Comfort and disarray,
Hard and easy...

Enough is enough,
will always be enough.

"He who knows enough is enough will always have enough"

NORTH

"Even the sage is unsure of this"

_____ !

Awakening

Enjoy

Stay with it

Be safe Be seen

Presence

Ultimate Medicine

_____ !

**No body
No here**

**No here
No body**

Therefore

The ancients say

**"Form is emptiness
Emptiness is form"**

-Buddha

Awakening

**Below no move
Unless
Awaken**

**Even
Cloud return
To ground**

Therefore

The ancients say

**"The wise confronts difficulty
before difficulty confronts the wise"**

-Tao Te Ching

Enjoy

**Entry to exit
Exit to entry**

Is there third option?

Therefore

The ancients say

"She let's go of that and enjoys this"

-   Tao Te Ching

Stay with it

**If problem dealt with before begin
Solution get no credit**

**If old problem is dealt with before
begin again
One would need no repeat medicine**

**And if one needs repeat medicine
Then it'll likely begin again**

**Therefore
The ancients say**

**"It not strive yet overcomes
It not speak yet answers
It not ask yet fulfills
It at ease yet follows a plan"**

-Tao Te Ching

Be safe Be seen

See self
Safe from self

See others
Safe from others

Therefore

The ancients say

"Seeing the small is insight"

-Tao Te Ching

Presence

If you alone
Are you really all alone?

When you with all
Are you also not alone?

Therefore

The ancients say

"Hidden deep but ever present"

- Tao Te Ching

Ultimate Medicine

Medicine and no need for it

Come from same source

The mystery within the mystery

Therefore

The ancients say

"Even the sage is unsure of this"

- Tao Te Ching

"Hidden deep but ever present"

www.ingramcontent.com/pod-product-compliance
Lightning Source LLC
Chambersburg PA
CBHW070326100426
42743CB00011B/2571